COOKING WITH
HERBS

Valerie Ferguson

LORENZ BOOKS

Contents

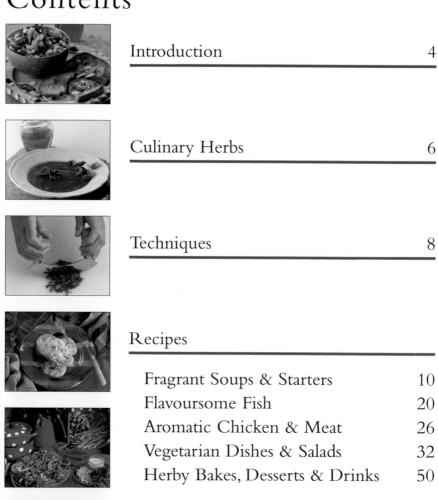

Introduction

Herbs are, simply, edible plants whose leaves have a particularly strong flavour or aroma when they are crushed or heated. It is usual to use just the leaves stripped from coarse stalks, but occasionally softer stalks and flowers are used too.

By far the best way to use herbs is straight from the garden. You'll find they can be grown in a comparatively small area and, given a sunny position, most will thrive in poor soils; failing that, pot a few up and stand on a brightly lit windowsill. Herbs such as bay, rosemary and thyme are evergreens and can be picked all year round.

Supermarkets now offer an increasing selection of pot-grown or prepacked fresh herbs. These are fine, especially out of season when there is little available from the garden; however, they can be soft and do not have the robust flavour of a freshly picked garden crop.

Dried herbs are also useful in winter, but a number lose their flavour and acquire hay-like overtones during drying and storage. Choose freeze-dried brands for the best flavour and store in airtight containers in a dark cupboard. Glass jars on a brightly lit spice rack may look attractive, but are not ideal for the purpose.

Culinary Herbs

There is a vast range of wonderful, aromatic herbs used to add flavour in cooking. Here is just a small sample of the most popular and versatile.

BAY

This has dark green, leathery leaves which are generally used whole to impart a delicate flavour to sauces. To increase the flavour crush the leaf in your hand or tear into pieces. It is an essential component of a bouquet garni.

CHERVIL

A very delicate herb with soft, lacy, fern-like leaves. It has a very mild aniseed flavour so use plenty of it and add only near the end of cooking.

CHIVES

These have slender, cylindrical, grass-like leaves with a mild onion flavour. Use fresh with egg and cheese dishes or in salads.

CORIANDER/ CILANTRO

With its finely scalloped, broad leaf, coriander (cilantro) has a spicy, pungent flavour. Leaves and stalks can be used, particularly fresh in salsas. It works well with fish dishes and is essential in Indian recipes.

DILL

A distinctive, pungent herb with blue-green, feathery leaves. It goes well with fish and egg dishes and also cream sauces.

GARLIC

A strongly flavoured member of the onion family, garlic can perhaps claim to be the cook's most indispensable kitchen ingredient. It adds pungency in its raw state and yet is wonderfully creamy if baked, roasted or used in a casserole. Add a little salt to raw garlic to bring out its wonderful flavour. For a less pungent taste, try increasing the cooking time. The pinkish-purple cloves are considered to have the best flavour.

OREGANO & MARJORAM

These herbs are from the same family. They both have small, oval, peppery-flavoured leaves which enhance tomato-based sauces. Oregano has a more robust flavour than sweeter marjoram.

MINT

Well-known for its freshly flavoured, bright green leaves. Traditionally used with lamb, it works well with fish and some vegetable dishes. It also adds a refreshing note to many desserts. It is used widely in Mediterranean and middle-eastern cuisine.

PARSLEY

Two varieties of this widely used herb are available: curly parsley and flat-leaf parsley. Flat-leaf parsley has a more concentrated flavour, but curly parsley is more easily chopped. If using parsley in a marinade, stock or bouquet garni, use most of the stalk as this has a stronger flavour. It is also a useful garnish for many dishes.

ROSEMARY

This herb has aromatic, needle-like leaves. They are coarse and pungent, so use sparingly and chop very finely. It is one of the herbs which can be picked all-year-round and is therefore useful for winter cooking when tender herbs are in short supply.

TARRAGON

With its long, narrow, glossy leaves and warm, aniseed flavour, tarragon is an essential sauce flavouring. Use fresh French tarragon rather than Russian or dried tarragon.

THYME

This herb has tiny, oval leaves with a strong flavour which works well with most dishes. Some varieties have a lemon scent which is a fine complement to chicken and fish recipes. It is coarse, so remove the leaves from the stalks. Along with bay leaves and sage, thyme is a key component of the traditional bouquet garni, used to flavour stocks and casseroles.

Techniques

HARVESTING & DRYING

Herbs are bountiful, putting on rapid growth during the summer months, so there is plenty to harvest for culinary use over the summer and an abundance in autumn when the season is over. In fact, herbs benefit from a certain amount of harvesting during their summer growing period. It is best to keep pinching out the tops to encourage bushiness and to stop flowers from forming. Collecting herbs for the cooking pot therefore can benefit the plant – provided you do not denude it. However, if you would like to enjoy the flowers on your herbs, allow some plants to bloom while pinching out others for use in the kitchen.

Herbs are best harvested in mid-morning, after the dew has dried, but before the aroma has been dissipated by the hot sun. Use sharp secateurs and, if you are harvesting during the growing season, aim to improve the shape of the plant by taking stems that have grown over-long. Herbs are lovely used fresh, and during the summer you will probably prefer to harvest just as you need them. By the beginning of autumn, the herbs are more or less over and will need to be cut down. This is the time for the major harvest. As you cut them, make them into small bunches using elastic bands. You can use string if you like, but elastic bands are better because they tighten round the herb stalks as they dry. The bunches should then be hung upside-down to dry in a well-ventilated, damp-free room. To make bouquets garnis, wrap either a single variety or a selection of dried leaves in small squares of muslin and tie with cotton string.

Many culinary herbs blend perfectly together; for bouquets garnis gather the various ingredients at the same time and mix together in small bunches, as they are easier to assemble while fresh.

Hang your herbs upside-down in a dry, airy place, out of direct sunlight. Once they are dry, wrap them up in plain, brown paper.

CHOPPING HERBS
Chop fresh herbs just before you need to add them to a dish.

Remove and discard any thick stalks, then use a sharp knife to chop the leaves finely. This should be done as close to the cooking or eating time as possible to prevent the leaves from discolouring.

Alternatively, use a herb chopper, also called a mezzaluna. Move the blade from side to side in a rocking motion.

FREEZING & DRYING HERBS
Fresh herbs can be preserved both in the freezer and by air-drying.

To freeze herbs divide them into small, equal amounts and put each one in a section of an icc-cube tray. Cover with cold water and place in the freezer. Fresh herbs preserved in this way lose little of their flavour.

To dry herbs either hang them upside down in bunches or arrange individual leaves separately on racks. Both methods require a well-ventilated, dry environment.

Tomato & Fresh Basil Soup

A delicious soup for late summer when fresh tomatoes and basil are in abundance and at their most flavoursome.

Serves 4–6

INGREDIENTS

15 ml/1 tbsp olive oil
25 g/1 oz/2 tbsp butter
1 medium onion, finely chopped
900 g/2 lb ripe Italian plum tomatoes,
    roughly chopped
1 garlic clove, roughly chopped
about 750 ml/1¼ pints/3 cups chicken
    or vegetable stock
120 ml/4 fl oz/½ cup dry white wine
30 ml/2 tbsp sun-dried tomato purée (paste)
30 ml/2 tbsp shredded fresh basil,
    plus a few whole leaves to garnish
150 ml/¼ pint/⅔ cup double (heavy) cream
salt and freshly ground black pepper

1 Heat the oil and butter in a large pan until foaming. Add the onion and cook gently for about 5 minutes, stirring frequently, until softened but not brown.

2 Stir in the chopped tomatoes and garlic, stir until well coated with the oil and butter, then add the stock, white wine and sun-dried tomato purée, with salt and pepper to taste. Stir to blend the ingredients, and bring to the boil. Lower the heat, half-cover the pan and simmer gently for 20 minutes, stirring occasionally to stop the tomatoes sticking to the base of the pan.

3 Process the soup, with the shredded basil, in a blender or food processor until smooth, then press through a sieve (strainer) into a clean pan.

4 Add the double cream and heat through, stirring. Do not allow the soup to approach boiling point. Check the consistency and add more stock if necessary and then taste for seasoning. Pour into heated bowls and garnish with basil leaves. Serve at once.

VARIATION: The soup can also be served chilled for a refreshing summer alfresco lunch.

Wild Mushroom & Parsley Soup

This creamy soup, extra-tasty if made entirely with wild mushrooms, is given a special lift by the generous addition of chopped fresh parsley.

Serves 4

INGREDIENTS

50 g/2 oz/4 tbsp unsalted butter
4 shallots or 1 medium onion, chopped
450 g/1 lb wild mushrooms or a mixture
    of wild and cultivated mushrooms,
    trimmed and chopped
1 garlic clove, crushed
900 ml/1½ pints/3¾ cups hot
    chicken stock,
60 ml/4 tbsp double (heavy) cream
30 ml/2 tbsp lemon juice
salt and freshly ground black pepper
45ml/3 tbsp chopped fresh parsley

1 Melt the butter in a pan, add the shallots or onion and soften over a gentle heat.

2 Add the mushrooms and garlic, and fry gently until the mushrooms soften and the juices begin to run.

3 Add the chicken stock, bring to the boil and simmer uncovered for 15 minutes. Liquidize until smooth and return to the saucepan.

4 Stir in the double cream, sharpen with lemon juice, then season with salt and freshly ground black pepper to taste. Ladle into four warmed soup bowls, scatter with the chopped parsley and serve.

Tuscan Bean & Herb Soup

There are lots of versions of this wonderful soup. This one uses cannellini beans, leeks, cabbage, fresh herbs and good-quality olive oil – and tastes even better reheated.

Serves 4

INGREDIENTS
45 ml/3 tbsp extra-virgin olive oil
1 onion, roughly chopped
2 leeks, roughly chopped
1 large potato, peeled and diced
2 garlic cloves, finely chopped
1.2 litres/2 pints/5 cups vegetable stock
400 g/14 oz can cannellini beans, drained,
    liquid reserved
175 g/6 oz Savoy cabbage, shredded
45 ml/3 tbsp chopped fresh flat-leaf parsley
30 ml/2 tbsp chopped fresh oregano
75 g/3 oz/1 cup shaved Parmesan cheese
salt and freshly ground black pepper

FOR THE GARLIC TOASTS
30–45 ml/2–3 tbsp extra-virgin olive oil
4 thick slices country bread
1 garlic clove, peeled and bruised

1 Heat the oil in a large pan and gently cook the onion, leeks, potato and garlic for 4–5 minutes.

2 Pour on the vegetable stock and reserved liquid from the beans. Bring to the boil, cover and simmer for 15 minutes.

3 Stir in the cabbage and beans, with half the parsley and oregano, season and cook for 10 minutes more. Spoon about one third of the soup into a food processor or blender and process until fairly smooth. Return to the soup in the pan, taste for seasoning and heat through for a further 5 minutes.

4 Meanwhile, make the garlic toasts. Drizzle a little oil over the slices of bread, then rub both sides of each slice with the garlic. Toast until browned on both sides. Keep them warm in a low oven. Ladle the soup into bowls. Sprinkle with the remaining parsley and oregano and the Parmesan shavings. Add a drizzle of olive oil and serve with the toasts.

Carrot & Coriander Soufflés

Use tender young carrots for this light-as-air dish.

Serves 4

INGREDIENTS
450 g/1 lb carrots
30 ml/2 tbsp chopped fresh coriander
   (cilantro)
4 eggs, separated
salt and freshly ground black pepper

1 Peel the carrots. Cook them in boiling, salted water for 20 minutes or until completely tender. Drain, then process until smooth in a food processor.

2 Preheat the oven to 200°C/400°F Gas 6. Season the puréed carrots with salt and freshly ground pepper, and stir in the chopped coriander.

3 Fold the egg yolks into the carrot mixture and blend well. In a separate bowl, whisk the egg whites until stiff.

4 Carefully fold the egg whites into the carrot mixture and pour into four small, greased ramekins. Bake for about 20 minutes or until risen and golden. Serve immediately.

A Quartet of Herby Cheeses

These fragrant cheeses are perfect served with Thyme & Mustard Biscuits.

Dill & Pink Peppercorn Cheese

Put 150 g/5 oz of "mild" goat's cheese on a plate. Finely chop some fresh dill and mix with 2.5 ml/½ tsp crushed pink peppercorns. Sprinkle over the cheese and press with the back of a spoon until lightly coated. Wrap in squares of waxed paper or baking parchment and chill. Use within 3 days.

Thyme & Chopped Garlic Cheese

Put 100 g/3¾ oz round of full fat goat's cheese on a plate. Mix 1 tablespoon of fresh thyme leaves and flowers with a finely chopped garlic clove and press them over the cheese. Wrap and store as described above.

Minted Feta

Cut the wrapper off a 200 g/7 oz pack of feta cheese, drain and cut into small dice. Finely chop a small bunch of fresh mint leaves, then roll the cubes of feta cheese in the fresh mint until lightly coated. Wrap and store as described left.

Tarragon & Lemon Cheese

Weigh out 200 g/7 oz of low-fat soft (farmer's) cheese, put on to a plate and cut into two squares. Tear the leaves off a small bunch of fresh tarragon, finely chop and use to coat the two squares of cheese. Sprinkle with the finely grated rind of ½ lemon or make rind curls using a lemon zester. Wrap and store as described left.

Clockwise from left: dill and pink peppercorn, tarragon and lemon, minted feta, and thyme and chopped garlic cheese.

Feta & Herb Filo Parcels

Versions of these crisp, cheese-and-herb-filled pastries are a common feature of street food throughout much of the Mediterranean. They are easy to make at home, but require a little time and patience.

Makes 10

INGREDIENTS
250 g/9 oz feta cheese, crumbled
2.5 ml/½ tsp grated nutmeg
30 ml/2 tbsp each, chopped fresh
 parsley, dill and mint
10 filo pastry sheets, each about
 30 x 18 cm/12 x 7 in
75 g/3 oz/6 tbsp melted butter or
 90 ml/6 tbsp olive oil
freshly ground black pepper

1 Preheat the oven to 190°C/375°F/ Gas 5. Mix the feta, nutmeg and herb filling in a large bowl. Add pepper to taste and mix to a smooth, creamy filling.

2 Brush 5 sheets of filo pastry lightly with melted butter or oil. Place another filo sheet on top of each and brush these too.

3 Cut the buttered sheets in half lengthways to make 10 strips, each 30 x 9 cm/12 x 3½ in. Place 5 ml/ 1 tsp of the cheese filling at the end of a long strip, fold the corners in diagonally to enclose it, then roll the pastry up into a cigar shape.

4 Brush the end with a little butter or oil to seal, then place join side down on a non-stick baking sheet. Repeat with the remaining pastry and filling. Brush the parcels with more butter or oil and bake for 20 minutes or until golden. Cool on a wire rack and serve at room temperature.

COOK'S TIP: When using filo pastry, it is important to keep unused sheets covered so that they don't dry out. The quantities used in the recipe above are approximate, as the size of filo sheets varies.

Fillets of Haddock Baked with Thyme & Garlic

Quick cooking is the essence of this dish. Use the freshest garlic available and half the amount of dried thyme if fresh is not available.

Serves 4

INGREDIENTS
4 haddock fillets, about 175 g/6 oz each
1 shallot, finely chopped
2 garlic cloves,
    thinly sliced
4 sprigs fresh thyme,
    plus extra to garnish
grated rind and juice of
    1 lemon
30 ml/2 tbsp extra-virgin olive oil
salt and freshly ground
    black pepper

2 Season well with salt and freshly ground black pepper.

3 Drizzle over the lemon juice and oil and bake for about 15 minutes. Serve scattered with finely grated lemon rind and garnished with thyme.

1 Preheat the oven to 180°C/350°F/ Gas 4. Lay the haddock fillets in the base of a large roasting tin or dish. Scatter the shallot, garlic cloves and thyme sprigs on top.

VARIATION: If haddock is not available, you can use cod or other firm white fish fillets for this recipe. You can also use a mixture of fresh herbs rather than just thyme.

Cod, Basil & Tomato with a Potato Thatch

Fresh herbs make all the difference to this fish pie which, served with a green salad, makes an ideal dish for lunch or a family supper.

Serves 8

INGREDIENTS
1 kg/2¼ lb smoked cod
1 kg/2¼ lb white cod
about 900 ml/1½ pints/3¾ cups milk
2 sprigs fresh basil
1 sprig fresh lemon thyme
150 g/5 oz/10 tbsp butter
1 onion, peeled and chopped
75 g/3 oz/⅓ cup flour
30 ml/2 tbsp tomato purée (paste)
30 ml/2 tbsp chopped fresh basil
12 medium-size old potatoes
salt and freshly ground black pepper
15 ml/1 tbsp chopped fresh parsley

2 Carefully flake the fish and set aside. Melt 75 g/3 oz/6 tbsp of the butter in a pan, add the onion and gently cook for 5 minutes, until tender. Add the flour, tomato purée and half the chopped basil. Add the fish cooking liquid, plus a little more milk if necessary, to make a fairly thin sauce.

3 Bring to the boil, season with salt and pepper and add the remaining chopped basil. Add the fish carefully and stir gently. Pour into an ovenproof dish.

1 Place both kinds of fish in a roasting tin with 600 ml/1 pint/2½ cups of the milk, 1.2 litres/2 pints/5 cups water and the basil and lemon thyme sprigs. Simmer for about 3–4 minutes. Leave to cool for about 20 minutes, then drain the fish, reserving the liquid.

4 Preheat the oven to 180°C/350°F/ Gas 4. Boil the potatoes in salted water until tender, then drain. Add the remaining butter and milk, and mash well. Season with salt and pepper. Spread the potatoes over the fish. Bake for 30 minutes. Serve with the chopped fresh parsley.

Salmon Steaks with Sorrel Sauce

Salmon and sorrel are traditionally paired in France.

Serves 2

INGREDIENTS
2 salmon steaks, about 250 g/9 oz each
5 ml/1 tsp olive oil
15 g/½ oz/1 tbsp butter
2 shallots, finely chopped
45 ml/3 tbsp whipping cream
90 g/3½ oz fresh sorrel or watercress leaves, washed and patted dry
salt and freshly ground black pepper
fresh sage, to garnish

1 Season the salmon steaks with salt and freshly ground black pepper. Brush a non-stick frying pan with the oil.

2 In a small pan, melt the butter and fry the shallots, stirring frequently, until softened. Add the cream and the sorrel, and cook until the sorrel is wilted, stirring constantly.

3 Heat the frying pan, add the salmon and cook for 5 minutes, turning once, until the flesh is opaque next to the bone and the juices run clear when pierced with a knife. Serve with the sage leaves and the sorrel sauce.

Grilled Red Mullet with Herbs

In Provence this fish is often charcoal-grilled with herbs.

Serves 4

INGREDIENTS
olive oil, for brushing
4 red mullet, about 225–275 g/8–10 oz each, cleaned and scaled
fresh herb sprigs, such as parsley, dill, basil or thyme
30–45 ml/2–3 tbsp pastis (anise liqueur)

1 About 1 hour before cooking, light a charcoal fire: when ready the coals should be grey with no flames. Generously brush a hinged grilling (broiling) rack with olive oil.

2 Brush each fish with a little olive oil and stuff the cavity with a few herb sprigs, breaking them to fit if necessary. Secure the fish in the grilling rack and grill (broil) for about 15–20 minutes, turning once during cooking.

3 Remove the fish to a warmed, flameproof serving dish. Pour the pastis into a small pan and heat for a moment or two, then tilt the pan and carefully ignite with a long match. Pour evenly over the red mullet and serve at once.

Roasted Spring Chicken with Fresh Herbs & Garlic

Thyme, sage, garlic and lemon are a classic combination.

Serves 4

INGREDIENTS
1.75 kg/4½ lb chicken or 4 poussins
finely grated rind and juice of 1 lemon
1 garlic clove, crushed
30 ml/2 tbsp olive oil
2 sprigs fresh thyme
2 sprigs fresh sage
75 g/3 oz/6 tbsp unsalted butter,
    softened
salt and freshly ground black pepper

1 Season the chicken or poussins. Mix the lemon rind and juice, garlic and olive oil together and pour over the chicken. Marinate for 2 hours in a non-metallic dish. Preheat the oven to 230°C/450°F/Gas 8.

2 Place the herbs in the cavity of the bird and smear the butter over the skin. Season well. Roast the chicken for 10 minutes, then turn the oven down to 190°C/375°F/Gas 5. Baste the chicken, and roast for 1 hour 30 minutes, until the juices run clear when the thigh is pierced. Rest for 15 minutes before carving.

Lemon & Rosemary Lamb Chops

Lamb is delicious with the fresh flavours of lemon and rosemary.

Serves 4

INGREDIENTS
12 spring lamb cutlets
45 ml/3 tbsp olive oil
2 large sprigs fresh rosemary,
    plus extra to garnish
juice of 1 lemon
3 garlic cloves, peeled
    and sliced
salt and freshly ground
    black pepper

1 Trim the excess fat from the lamb cutlets. Mix the oil, rosemary, lemon juice and garlic together until well blended and season to taste.

2 Pour the sauce over the chops in a shallow dish and marinate for 30 minutes. Preheat the grill (broiler) to a medium heat.

3 Remove the chops from the marinade and blot the excess with kitchen paper. Grill (broil) for about 10 minutes on each side, place on warmed serving plates, then serve garnished with rosemary sprigs.

Pork Fillet with Sage & Orange

Sage is often partnered with pork – there seems to be a natural affinity. The addition of orange brings sophistication and balances the sometimes overpowering flavour of sage.

Serves 4

INGREDIENTS
2 pork fillets, about 350 g/12 oz each
15 g/½ oz/1 tbsp butter
120 ml/4 fl oz/½ cup dry sherry
175 ml/6 fl oz/¾ cup chicken stock
2 garlic cloves, very finely chopped
grated rind and juice of 1 unwaxed orange
3 or 4 fresh sage leaves, finely chopped
10 ml/2 tsp cornflour (cornstarch)
salt and freshly ground black pepper
orange wedges and sage leaves,
    to garnish

1 Season the pork fillets lightly with salt and pepper. Melt the butter in a heavy, flameproof casserole over a medium-high heat, then add the meat and cook for 5–6 minutes, turning to brown all sides evenly. Add the sherry, boil for about 1 minute, then add the stock, garlic, orange rind and sage.

2 Bring to the boil and reduce the heat to low, then cover and simmer for 20 minutes, turning once until the juices run clear when the meat is pierced with a knife, or when a meat thermometer inserted into the thickest part of the meat registers 66°C/150°F. Transfer the pork to a warmed platter and cover to keep warm.

3 Bring the sauce to the boil. Blend the cornflour and orange juice and stir into the sauce, then boil gently over a medium heat for a few minutes, stirring frequently, until the sauce is slightly thickened. Strain into a gravy boat or serving jug.

4 Slice the pork diagonally and pour the meat juices into the sauce. Spoon a little sauce over the pork and garnish with orange wedges and sage leaves. Serve the remaining sauce separately.

Traditional Beef Stew & Herb Dumplings

This aromatic dish can cook slowly in the oven while you go for a wintery walk to work up an appetite.

Serves 6

INGREDIENTS
25 g/1 oz/¼ cup plain (all-purpose) flour
1.2 kg/2½ lb stewing steak, cubed
30 ml/2 tbsp olive oil
2 large onions, sliced
450 g/1 lb carrots, sliced
300 ml/½ pint/1¼ cups Guinness or
   dark beer
3 bay leaves
10 ml/2 tsp brown sugar
3 sprigs fresh thyme
5 ml/1 tsp cider vinegar
salt and freshly ground black pepper

FOR THE DUMPLINGS
115 g/4 oz/½ cup grated hard white fat
225 g/8 oz/2 cups self-raising (self-rising)
   flour
30 ml/2 tbsp chopped mixed fresh herbs
about 150 ml/¼ pint/⅔ cup water

1 Preheat the oven to 160°C/325°F/ Gas 3. Season the flour and sprinkle over the steak, tossing to coat well.

2 Heat the oil in a large flameproof casserole dish and lightly sauté the onions and carrots for 5 minutes until just softening. Remove the onions and carrots from the dish with a slotted spoon and reserve them.

3 Brown the meat well in batches in the casserole dish.

4 Return all the vegetables to the casserole and add any leftover seasoned flour. Add the Guinness or beer, bay leaves, sugar and thyme. Bring the liquid to the boil and then transfer to the oven. Leave the meat to cook for 1 hour 40 minutes before making the dumplings.

5 Mix the grated fat, flour and herbs together. Add enough water to make a soft, sticky dough and form it into small balls with floured hands.

6 Add the cider vinegar to the meat and spoon the dumplings on top. Cook the stew for a further 20 minutes, until the dumplings have cooked through, and serve hot.

Linguine with Basil Pesto Sauce

Pesto originates in Liguria, where the sea breezes are said to give the local basil a particularly fine flavour. It is traditionally made with a pestle and mortar, but using a food processor or blender is easier.

Serves 5–6

INGREDIENTS
65 g/2½ oz/¾ cup fresh
   basil leaves
3–4 garlic cloves, peeled
45 ml/3 tbsp pine nuts
2.5 ml/½ tsp salt
75 ml/5 tbsp olive oil
50 g/2 oz/⅔ cup grated
   Parmesan cheese
60 ml/4 tbsp finely grated
   pecorino cheese
freshly ground black pepper
500 g/1¼ lb linguine

2 Stir in the Parmesan and pecorino cheeses. Taste the sauce and adjust the seasoning as necessary.

3 Cook the pasta in a large pan of rapidly boiling, salted water until it is al dente. Just before draining it, take about 60 ml/4 tbsp of the cooking water and stir it into the sauce.

1 Place the basil, garlic, pine nuts, salt and olive oil in a blender or food processor, and process until smooth, or blend using a pestle and mortar if preferred. Remove to a bowl.

4 Drain the pasta and toss with the sauce. Serve immediately.

Garlic & Herb Pasta

A tasty pasta dish served with plenty of fresh herbs and Parmesan cheese, this makes a speedy and satisfying supper.

Serves 4

INGREDIENTS
250 g/9 oz mixed egg and
    spinach tagliatelle
3 garlic cloves, crushed
30 ml/2 tbsp drained bottled capers,
    finely chopped
5 ml/1 tsp Dijon mustard
50 ml/2 fl oz/¼ cup olive oil
60 ml/4 tbsp chopped mixed fresh
    chives, parsley and oregano
50 g/2 oz/⅓ cup pine nuts, toasted
15 ml/1 tbsp fresh lemon juice
salt and freshly ground
    black pepper
shaved Parmesan cheese,
    to serve

2 Using a pestle and mortar, pound the garlic until smooth or put through a garlic press. Transfer to a large bowl, add the capers and mustard, and mix well.

3 Gradually drizzle in the olive oil, mixing until thoroughly combined. Stir in the chives, parsley and oregano, toasted pine nuts and fresh lemon juice. Season well to taste.

4 Drain the pasta and toss together with the herb dressing, until well combined. Serve sprinkled with plenty of shaved Parmesan cheese.

1 Cook the pasta in plenty of boiling, salted water in a large pan, according to the packet instructions, until just tender but retaining a bit of bite.

VARIATION: Other pasta shapes such as penne or farfalle (bows) can be used for this quick dish.

Fresh Herb Pizza

Cut this pizza into thin wedges and serve as part of mixed antipasti.

Serves 8

INGREDIENTS
115 g/4 oz/2 cups mixed fresh herbs,
    such as parsley, basil and oregano
3 garlic cloves, crushed
120 ml/4 fl oz/½ cup double (heavy)
    cream
1 ready-made pizza base,
    25–30 cm/10–12 in diameter
15 ml/1 tbsp olive oil
115 g/4 oz/1 cup finely grated pecorino
    cheese
salt and freshly ground black pepper

3 Place the pizza base on a baking
sheet or terracotta pizza stone.
Brush with the olive oil, then spread
over the herb mixture.

1 Preheat the oven to 220°C/425°F/
Gas 7. Finely chop the herbs, using
a food processor if you have one, and
place in a bowl.

2 Add the garlic, cream and seasoning
to the bowl and mix together
thoroughly.

4 Sprinkle over the pecorino cheese.
Bake for 15–20 minutes, until the
base is crisp and golden and the
topping is still moist. Cut into thin
wedges and serve immediately.

COOK'S TIP: As part of varied
Italian antipasti, serve the pizza
wedges with bowls of green and
black olives, and toasted ciabatta
bread spread with pesto and shreds
of fresh basil.

Pepper & Oregano Gratin

Serve this simple but delicious dish as a starter with a small mixed-leaf or rocket (arugula) salad and some good, crusty bread to mop up the delicious juices from the roasted peppers.

Serves 4

INGREDIENTS
2 red (bell) peppers
30 ml/2 tbsp extra-virgin
    olive oil
60 ml/4 tbsp fresh white breadcrumbs
1 garlic clove, finely chopped
5 ml/1 tsp drained bottled capers
8 stoned black olives,
    roughly chopped
15 ml/1 tbsp chopped fresh oregano
15 ml/1 tbsp chopped fresh
    flat-leaf parsley
salt and freshly ground black pepper
fresh herbs, to garnish

2 Peel the peppers. (Don't skin them under the tap as the water would wash away some of the flavour.) Halve them, discard the seeds and cut the flesh into large strips.

3 Use a little of the olive oil to grease a small baking dish. Arrange the pepper strips in the dish.

4 Scatter the remaining ingredients on top, drizzle with the rest of the olive oil and add salt and pepper to taste. Bake for about 20 minutes, until the breadcrumbs have browned. Serve, garnished with fresh herbs.

1 Preheat the oven to 200°C/400°F/ Gas 6. Place the peppers under a hot grill (broiler). Turn occasionally until they are blackened and blistered all over. Remove from the heat and place in a plastic bag. Seal and leave to cool.

Baked Onions with Rosemary & Sun-dried Tomatoes

These little onions grow sweeter as they bake and become infused with the flavours of the fresh herbs and sun-dried tomatoes.

Serves 4

INGREDIENTS
butter, for greasing
450 g/1 lb button (pearl) onions
10 ml/2 tsp chopped fresh rosemary or
  3.5 ml/¾ tsp dried rosemary
2 garlic cloves, chopped
15 ml/1 tbsp chopped fresh parsley
120 ml/4 fl oz/½ cup sun-dried tomatoes
  in oil, drained and chopped
90 ml/6 tbsp olive oil
15 ml/1 tbsp white wine vinegar
salt and freshly ground black pepper
1 sprig fresh rosemary, to garnish

1 Preheat the oven to 150°C/300°F/ Gas 2. Lightly grease a shallow baking dish. Drop the onions into a pan of boiling water and cook for 5 minutes. Drain well.

2 Spread the onions in the bottom of the prepared baking dish.

3 Combine the rosemary, garlic, parsley, salt and black pepper and sprinkle over the onions.

4 Scatter the sun-dried tomatoes over the herbs and onions. Drizzle the olive oil over and sprinkle the white wine vinegar on top.

5 Cover with a sheet of foil and bake for 45 minutes, basting occasionally. Remove the foil and bake for about 15 minutes longer, until the onions are golden. Garnish with a sprig of fresh rosemary and serve.

Garden Salad with Herbs & Flowers

You can use any fresh, edible flowers for this beautiful salad.

Serves 4

INGREDIENTS
1 cos lettuce
175 g/6 oz rocket (arugula)
1 small frisée lettuce
sprigs of fresh chervil and tarragon
15 ml/1 tbsp snipped fresh chives
handful of mixed edible flower heads,
    such as nasturtiums or marigolds

FOR THE DRESSING
45 ml/3 tbsp olive oil
15 ml/1 tbsp white wine vinegar
2.5 ml/½ tsp French mustard
1 garlic clove, crushed
pinch of sugar

1 Mix the cos, rocket and frisée leaves and herbs together.

2 Make the dressing by whisking all the ingredients together in a large bowl. Toss the salad leaves in the bowl with the dressing, add the flower heads and serve at once.

Tomato, Savory & French Bean Salad

A superb accompaniment for all cold meats or vegetable salads.

Serves 4

INGREDIENTS
500 g/1¼ lb green beans
1 kg/2¼ lb ripe tomatoes
3 spring onions (scallions),
    roughly sliced
15 ml/1 tbsp pine nuts
6–8 sprigs fresh savory

FOR THE DRESSING
30 ml/2 tbsp extra-virgin
    olive oil
juice of 1 lime
75 g/3 oz Dolcelatte cheese
1 garlic clove, peeled and crushed
salt and freshly ground black pepper

1 Prepare the dressing first so that it can stand a while before use. Place all the dressing ingredients in the bowl of a food processor, season to taste and blend until all the cheese has been finely chopped and you have a smooth dressing. Pour it into a jug.

2 Top and tail the beans, and boil in salted water until just cooked. Drain and refresh under cold water. Slice the tomatoes, or quarter them, if small.

3 Toss the beans, tomatoes and spring onions together. Pour on the salad dressing. Sprinkle the pine nuts over the top, followed by the savory.

Brown Bean & Thyme Salad

Brown beans, sometimes called "ful medames", are widely used in Egyptian cookery. Black or red kidney beans make a good substitute.

Serves 6

INGREDIENTS
350 g/12 oz/1¾ cups dried brown beans
3 sprigs fresh thyme
2 bay leaves
1 onion, halved
4 garlic cloves, crushed
7.5 ml/1½ tsp cumin seeds,
    crushed
3 spring onions (scallions),
    finely chopped
90 ml/6 tbsp chopped fresh parsley
20 ml/4 tsp lemon juice
90 ml/6 tbsp olive oil
3 hard-boiled eggs, shelled and
    roughly chopped
1 pickled cucumber, roughly chopped
salt and freshly ground black pepper

1 Soak the beans overnight in plenty of cold water. Drain, transfer to a large pan and cover with fresh water. Bring to the boil and boil rapidly for 10 minutes.

2 Reduce the heat and add the thyme, bay leaves and onion. Simmer very gently for about 1 hour, until tender. Drain and discard the herbs and onion.

3 Mix together the garlic, cumin, spring onions, parsley, lemon juice and oil and add a little salt and pepper. Pour over the beans and toss the ingredients lightly together. Gently stir in the eggs and cucumber and serve at once with crusty bread.

Yogurt & Herb Dip

This refreshing dish, made with cooling cucumber, is called Cacik or Tzatziki in the Mediterranean.

Serves 6

INGREDIENTS
1 small cucumber
300 ml/½ pint/1¼ cups thick
    natural (plain) yogurt
3 garlic cloves, crushed
30 ml/2 tbsp chopped fresh mint
30 ml/2 tbsp chopped fresh dill or parsley
salt and freshly ground black pepper
mint or dill, and parsley, to garnish
olive oil, olives and pitta bread, to serve

1 Finely chop the cucumber and layer in a colander with plenty of salt. Leave for 30 minutes. Wash the cucumber in several changes of cold water and drain thoroughly. Pat dry on kitchen paper.

2 Mix together the yogurt, garlic and herbs, and season with salt and pepper. Stir in the cucumber. Garnish with fresh herbs, drizzle over a little olive oil and serve with olives and pitta bread.

Herbal Oils & Vinegars

Capture the very essence of herbs in oils and vinegars, which you can use in your cooking.

Pour extra-virgin olive oil or vinegar into a sterilized wide-topped jar and add a large handful of herbs. Steep for two weeks, then strain and decant into a sterile bottle. Add a few sprigs of fresh, moisture-free herbs to indicate the flavour of the oil or vinegar. Store out of direct sunlight and use within two weeks of bottling.

Above: Finish off the bottles by neatly winding cotton string around a wax paper top and tying it securely with a reef knot.

Mixed Herb Oil

Steep sage, rosemary, tarragon and marjoram in extra-virgin olive oil according to the instructions above, then decant. Use to pan-fry chicken or make into herby salad dressings.

Dill & Lemon Oil

Steep a handful of fresh dill and a large strip of lemon rind in extra-virgin olive oil according to the instructions above, then decant. Add 2 large fronds dill and 2 strips lemon peel to the bottle. Use to pan-fry or grill fish.

Thyme Oil

Steep a handful of thyme in extra-virgin olive oil as above, then decant. Add 2 sprigs thyme to the bottle for decoration. Excellent for chicken.

Mediterranean Herb Oil

Steep fresh rosemary, thyme and marjoram in extra-virgin olive oil according to the instructions above, then decant. Decorate with herbs tied around a cinnamon stick. Add to enhance garlicky tomato sauces, coq au vin or lamb daubes.

Basil & Chilli Oil

Steep basil and 3 chillies in extra-virgin olive oil according to the instructions above, then decant. Put 2 sprigs basil and 3 chillies in the bottle to decorate. Add to tomato and mozzarella salads. This oil is particularly delicious brushed over Italian-style breads.

Rosemary & Red Wine Vinegar

Steep rosemary in red wine vinegar according to the instructions left, then decant and add a few long stems of rosemary, plus some pink rose petals.

Above: Beautiful and delicious, herbal oils make exquisite gifts. From left to right: basil and chilli, Mediterranean herb, dill and lemon, thyme, and mixed herb.

Mixed Herb Vinegar

Steep sage, thyme, bay and marjoram in white wine vinegar as described left, then decant. Tie a selection of the herbs with string. Insert into the bottle for identification.

Tarragon Vinegar

Steep tarragon in cider vinegar as described left, then decant. Insert 3 long sprigs of tarragon.

Herb Garden Dressing

This dried mixture will keep through the winter until your herbs are growing again. It can be used to flavour hot or cold dishes.

Makes about
500 g/1¼ lb/4¼ cups

INGREDIENTS

115 g/4 oz/1 cup dried oregano
115 g/4 oz/1 cup dried basil
50 g/2 oz/½ cup dried marjoram
50 g/2 oz/½ cup dried dill
50 g/2 oz/½ cup dried mint leaves
50 g/2 oz/½ cup onion powder
30 ml/2 tbsp dry English mustard
10 ml/2 tsp salt
15 ml/1 tbsp freshly ground black pepper

1 Mix the ingredients together in a jar or whisk in a bowl, and keep in a sealed, sterile jar to use as needed.

2 When making a batch of salad dressing, take 30 ml/2 tbsp of the herb mixture and add it to 350 ml/ 12 fl oz/1½ cups extra-virgin olive oil and 120 ml/4 fl oz/½ cup cider vinegar. Mix thoroughly and allow to stand for 1 hour. Mix again and taste to check seasoning before using.

Coriander Pesto Salsa

This aromatic salsa is delicious drizzled over fish and chicken, tossed with pasta ribbons or used to dress a fresh avocado and tomato salad.

Serves 4

INGREDIENTS
50 g/2 oz/1 cup fresh coriander (cilantro) leaves
15 g/½ oz/¼ cup fresh parsley
2 red chillies
1 garlic clove
50 g/2 oz/⅓ cup shelled pistachio nuts
25 g/1 oz/⅓ cup Parmesan cheese, finely grated
90 ml/6 tbsp olive oil
juice of 2 limes
salt and freshly ground black pepper

1 Process the fresh herbs in a blender or food processor.

2 Halve the fresh chillies lengthways and remove their seeds, washing your hands afterwards. Add to the herbs, together with the garlic, and process until finely chopped.

3 Add the pistachio nuts to the herb mixture and pulse the power on the processor until they are roughly chopped. Transfer to an attractive serving bowl and stir in the Parmesan cheese, olive oil and fresh lime juice until well blended.

4 Add salt and freshly ground pepper to taste. Cover and chill the mixture until ready to serve.

Thyme & Mustard Biscuits

These aromatic, digestive-type biscuits are delicious served with one of the Herby Cheeses as a light, savoury last course.

Makes about 40

INGREDIENTS
175 g/6 oz/1½ cups wholemeal (whole-
  wheat) flour
50 g/2 oz/½ cup medium oatmeal
25 g/1 oz/2 tbsp caster (superfine) sugar
10 ml/2 tsp baking powder
30 ml/2 tbsp fresh thyme leaves
50 g/2 oz/4 tbsp butter
25 g/1 oz/2 tbsp white vegetable fat
45 ml/3 tbsp whole or
  semi-skimmed milk
10 ml/2 tsp Dijon mustard
30 ml/2 tbsp sesame seeds
salt and freshly ground black pepper

1 Preheat the oven to 200°C/400°F/
Gas 6. Sift the flour into a large
bowl, then add the oatmeal, sugar,
baking powder, fresh thyme leaves
and seasoning, and mix well. Cut the
fats into pieces and add to the bowl,
then rub in either with your
fingertips, lifting the mixture to
keep it cool, or a pastry cutter, to
form fine crumbs.

2 Mix the milk and mustard together
with a whisk until the mustard is
dissolved, stir into the flour mixture
and continue mixing until you have a
soft, but not sticky, dough. If the dough
seems too moist, add a little extra flour
until the right consistency is achieved.

3 Knead lightly on a floured surface,
then roll out to a thickness of
5 mm/¼ in. Stamp out 5 cm/2 in
rounds with a fluted biscuit cutter and
arrange, spaced slightly apart, on two
greased baking sheets. Reroll the
trimmings and continue stamping out
biscuits until all the dough is used.

4 Prick the biscuits with a fork and
sprinkle with sesame seeds. Bake
for 10–12 minutes until lightly
browned, alternating baking sheets on
the oven shelves during cooking for an
even colour. Cool on the trays, then
pack into a small biscuit tin. Store in a
cool place for up to 5 days.

VARIATION: You could use other
herbs such as rosemary or sage for
these savoury biscuits.

Rosemary Bread

This herb bread is delicious with cheese or soup for a light meal.

Makes 1 loaf

INGREDIENTS

7 g/¼ oz packet easy-blend dried yeast
175 g/6 oz/1½ cups wholemeal (whole-
  wheat) flour
175 g/6 oz/1½ cups self-raising (self-rising)
  flour
50 ml/2 fl oz/¼ cup warm water
250 ml/8 fl oz/1 cup whole or semi-skimmed
  milk (room temperature)
15 ml/1 tbsp sugar
25 g/1 oz/2 tbsp butter, melted,
  plus extra for greasing
5 ml/1 tsp salt
15 ml/1 tbsp sesame seeds
15 ml/1 tbsp dried chopped onion
15 ml/1 tbsp fresh rosemary leaves,
  plus extra to decorate
115 g/4 oz/1 cup cubed Cheddar cheese
coarse salt, to decorate

2 Flatten the dough, then add the cheese cubes. Quickly knead them in until they are well-combined.

3 Place the dough in a clean bowl greased with a little butter, turning it so that it becomes greased on all sides. Cover with a clean, dry cloth. Put the bowl in a warm place for about 1½ hours or until the dough has risen and doubled in size.

4 Grease a 23 x 13 cm/9 x 5 in loaf tin with butter. Knock down the dough and shape it into a loaf. Put the loaf into the tin, cover with the clean cloth and leave for about 1 hour, until doubled in size. Preheat the oven to 190°C/375°F/Gas 5.

1 Mix the yeast with the flours in a large mixing bowl. Stir in the warm water, milk, sugar, butter, salt, sesame seeds, onion and rosemary. Knead thoroughly until quite smooth.

5 Bake the loaf for 30 minutes. During the last 5–10 minutes of cooking time, cover it with foil to prevent it from becoming too dark. Remove from the tin and cool on a wire rack. Decorate with rosemary leaves and coarse salt.

Cheese & Marjoram Scones

A great success for a hearty tea. With savoury toppings, these herb-flavoured scones can make a good basis for a light lunch, served with a crunchy, green salad.

Makes about 18 scones

INGREDIENTS
115 g/4 oz/1 cup wholemeal (whole-wheat)
   flour
115 g/4 oz/1 cup self-raising (self-rising)
   flour
pinch of salt
40 g/1½ oz/3 tbsp butter
1.5 ml/¼ tsp dry English mustard
10 ml/2 tsp dried marjoram
50–75 g/2–3 oz/½–¾ cup finely grated
   Cheddar cheese
120 ml/4 fl oz/½ cup milk, or as required
5 ml/1 tsp sunflower oil (optional)
50 g/2 oz/⅓ cup pecan nuts or
   walnuts, chopped

1 Gently sift the flours into a bowl and add the salt. Cut the butter into small pieces and rub these into the flour with your fingertips or use a pastry cutter, until the mixture resembles fine breadcrumbs.

2 Add the mustard, marjoram and grated cheese and mix in sufficient milk to make a soft dough. Knead the dough lightly.

3 Preheat the oven to 220°C/425°F/ Gas 7. Grease two baking trays with the paper from the butter (or use a little sunflower oil). Roll out the dough on a floured surface to about 2 cm/¾ in thickness and cut it out with a 5 cm/2 in square cutter. Place the squares on the baking trays.

4 Brush the squares with a little milk and sprinkle the chopped pecans or walnuts over the top. Bake for 12 minutes. Serve warm.

VARIATION: You could substitute a tablespoon of chopped fresh rosemary and hazelnuts if desired.

Lavender Cake

This summer-scented cake is
reminiscent of a country garden.

Serves 6–8

INGREDIENTS
175 g/6 oz/¾ cup unsalted butter, softened
175 g/6 oz/scant 1 cup caster (superfine)
 sugar
3 eggs, lightly beaten
175 g/6 oz/1½ cups self-raising (self-rising)
 flour, sifted
30 ml/2 tbsp fresh lavender florets or
 15 ml/1 tbsp dried culinary lavender,
 roughly chopped
2.5 ml/½ tsp vanilla essence
30 ml/2 tbsp milk
50 g/2 oz/½ cup icing (confectioners') sugar,
 sifted
2.5 ml/½ tsp water
a few fresh lavender florets, to decorate

1 Preheat the oven to 180°C/350°F/
 Gas 4. Lightly grease and flour a
ring tin (pan) or a deep 20 cm/8 in
round, loose-based cake tin. Cream the
butter and sugar together thoroughly.

2 Add the eggs gradually, between
 each addition, until the mixture
thickens. Fold in the flour, lavender,
vanilla essence and milk. Spoon the
mixture into the tin and bake for 1
hour. Leave for 5 minutes, then turn
out on to a wire rack to cool. Mix the
icing sugar with the water. Pour over
the cake and decorate with fresh
lavender florets.

Rose-petal Sorbet

This sorbet makes a wonderful end to a summer meal with its fabulous flavour of roses. Remember to use the most scented variety you can find in the garden. Pick fresh blooms which are newly opened.

Serves 4–6

INGREDIENTS
115g/4 oz caster (superfine) sugar
300 ml/½ pint/1¼ cups boiling water
petals of 3 large, scented red or deep pink
　　roses, white ends of petals removed
juice of 2 lemons
300 ml/½ pint/1¼ cups rosé wine
whole crystallized roses or rose petals,
　　to decorate

1 Place the sugar in a bowl and add the boiling water. Stir until the sugar has completely dissolved. Add the rose petals and leave to cool completely.

2 Blend the mixture in a food processor then strain through a sieve. Add the lemon juice and wine and pour into a freezer container. Freeze for several hours until the mixture has frozen around the edges.

3 Turn the sorbet into a mixing bowl and whisk until smooth. Re-freeze until frozen around the edges. Repeat the whisking and freezing process once or twice more, until the sorbet is pale and smooth. Freeze until firm.

4 Serve decorated with crystallized roses or rose petals.

COOK'S TIP: This sorbet can also be made in an ice cream maker. Churn the sorbet until firm, with a good texture.

Lemon Meringue Bombe with Mint Chocolate

This easy ice cream will cause a sensation at a dinner party – it is unusual, but quite the most delicious combination of tastes that you can imagine.

Serves 6–8

INGREDIENTS
2 large lemons
150 g/5 oz/¾ cup sugar
150 ml/¼ pint/⅔ cup whipping
    cream
600 ml/1 pint/2½ cups Greek natural
    (US strained plain) yogurt
2 large meringues
3 small sprigs fresh mint
225 g/8 oz good-quality
    mint chocolate, grated

2 Reserve 1 of the mint sprigs and chop the rest finely. Add to the cream and lemon mixture. Pour into a 1.2 litre/2 pint/5 cup glass pudding basin and cover with foil or clear wrap (plastic wrap) and freeze for 4 hours.

3 When the ice cream has frozen, scoop out the middle and pour in the grated mint chocolate, reserving a little for the decoration. Replace the ice cream so that it covers the mint chocolate, and refreeze for 3-4 hours.

1 Thinly pare the rind from the lemons, then squeeze the juice. Place the lemon rind and sugar in a food processor and blend well. Add the cream, yogurt and lemon juice and process until smooth. Pour the mixture into a mixing bowl and add the meringues, roughly crushed.

4 To turn out the bombe, dip the bottom of the basin in very hot water for a few seconds, to loosen the ice cream, then turn the basin upside down over a serving plate. Decorate the bombe with the reserved grated chocolate and sprig of mint.

Fragrant Herbal Drinks

Refreshing, cool drinks on a hot summer's day are all the more exotic for the secret ingredient of herbs. Whether you choose soft or alcoholic drinks, add a pretty touch by freezing flowers such as borage, in the ice cubes. For a summer party, serve refreshing fresh lemonade and delicious Pimm's.

Strawberry & Lavender Gin

The delicately perfumed quality of this drink makes it simply irresistible. It is perfect for a variety of summer celebrations in the garden, such as christenings, weddings and anniversaries.

Makes 1 bottle

INGREDIENTS
400 g/14 oz strawberries, hulled and
    thickly sliced
175 g/6 oz/scant 1 cup caster (superfine)
    sugar
8 large fresh lavender flowers
750 ml/1¼ pints/3 cups gin

1 Put the strawberries, sugar and lavender flowers into a large, wide-necked sterile jar. Pour on the gin and seal. Leave the jar in a cool place for 7 days, giving it a gentle shake each day.

VARIATION: You could experiment with other fruits such as raspberries, apricots or peaches.

2 Strain the gin off the fruit and lavender, then pour it back into the bottle, or into two smaller, more decorative bottles. Seal well. Store in a cool place for up to 4 months.

Pimm's with Borage

An attractive and most refreshing drink, to be served long, cool and garnished with pretty, blue borage flowers on hot summer days.

1 One-third fill a large jug or tall glasses with Pimm's No. 1. Add ice cubes and top up with chilled, fizzy lemonade or tonic water. Decorate with thinly sliced cucumber, halved orange slices, borage flowers and mint leaves.

From left to right: floral ice cubes, Pimm's and fresh lemonade.

Fresh Lemonade

Nothing matches home-made lemonade. Slightly sharp, it makes a most refreshing drink for both children and adults.

Makes about 24 glasses

INGREDIENTS
2½ lemons, thinly sliced
675 g/1½ lb/3½ cups sugar
1.2 litres/2 pints/5 cups water
25 g/1 oz/¼ cup citric acid
25 g/1 oz/½ cup fresh lemon balm
ice and chilled, still or sparkling mineral
    water, to serve

1 Put the sliced lemons in a large heavy pan or preserving pan with the sugar and water. Slowly bring to the boil, stirring occasionally until the sugar has dissolved. Boil for 15 minutes, then remove from the heat and stir in the citric acid. Add the lemon balm and leave to cool.

2 Discard the lemon balm and pour the lemonade into medium-size wide-necked sterile bottles. Seal and chill for up to 2 weeks.

3 To serve, pour the lemonade into a large jug until one-third full. Add ice and top with mineral water.

INDEX

This edition is published by Lorenz Books,
an imprint of Anness Publishing Ltd,
Blaby Road, Wigston, LE18 4SE

www.lorenzbooks.com; www.annesspublishing.com

If you like the images in this book and would like to investigate using them for publishing, promotions or advertising, please visit our website www.practicalpictures.com for more information.

Publisher: Joanna Lorenz
Editor: Valerie Ferguson & Helen Sudell
Series Designer: Bobbie Colgate Stone
Designer: Andrew Heath
Production Controller: Steve Lang

Recipes contributed by: Carla Capalbo, Frances Cleary, Carole Clements, Roz Denny, Nicola Diggins, Sarah Edmonds, Tessa Evelegh, Joanna Farrow, Silvano Franco, Shirley Gill, Katherine Richmond, Liz Trigg, Steven Wheeler, Elizabeth Wolf-Cohen

Photography: William Adams-Lingwood, Karl Adamson, James Duncan, John Freeman, Michelle Garrett, John Heseltine, Amanda Heywood, Janine Hosegood, Thomas Odulate, Debbie Patterson, Polly Wreford.

A CIP catalogue record for this book is available from the British Library

COOK'S NOTES

Bracketed terms are intended for American readers.

For all recipes, quantities are given in both metric and imperial measures and, where appropriate, in standard cups and spoons. Follow one set of measures, but not a mixture, because they are not interchangeable.

Standard spoon and cup measures are level. 1 tsp = 5ml, 1 tbsp = 15ml, 1 cup = 250ml/8fl oz. Australian standard tablespoons are 20ml. Australian readers should use 3 tsp in place of 1 tbsp for measuring small quantities.

American pints are 16fl oz/2 cups. American readers should use 20fl oz/2.5 cups in place of 1 pint when measuring liquids.

Electric oven temperatures in this book are for conventional ovens. When using a fan oven, the temperature will probably need to be reduced by about 10–20°C/20–40°F. Since ovens vary, you should check with your manufacturer's instruction book for guidance.

Medium (US large) eggs are used unless otherwise stated.

PUBLISHER'S NOTE:

Although the advice and information in this book are believed to be accurate and true at the time of going to press, neither the authors nor the publisher can accept any legal responsibility or liability for any errors or omissions that may arise from the use of this advice or information in this book.

© Anness Publishing Limited 2013